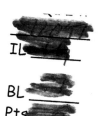

IL

BL
Pts

AR Quiz #

D1256656

On a Farm

by Cindy Chapman

Reading Consultant: Wiley Blevins, M.A.
Phonics/Early Reading Specialist

 COMPASS POINT BOOKS

Minneapolis, Minnesota

Compass Point Books
3109 West 50th Street, #115
Minneapolis, MN 55410

Visit Compass Point Books on the Internet at *www.compasspointbooks.com*
or e-mail your request to *custserv@compasspointbooks.com*

Photographs ©: Cover: PhotoDisc/PhotoLink/Scenics of America,
p. 1: PhotoDisc/PhotoLink/Scenics of America, p. 6: Corbis/Julie Habel,
p. 7: Bruce Coleman, Inc./Steve Solum, p. 8: Corbis/Joe Baraban,
p. 9: Minden Pictures/Konrad Wothe, p. 10: DigitalVision,
p. 11: Corbis/Frank Lane Picture Agency/John Watkins, p. 12: Corbis/Ariel Skelley

Editorial Development: Alice Dickstein, Alice Boynton
Photo Researcher: Wanda Winch
Design/Page Production: Silver Editions, Inc.

Library of Congress Cataloging-in-Publication Data
Chapman, Cindy.
  On a farm / Cindy Chapman.
    p. cm. — (Compass Point phonics readers)
Summary: Shows animals on a farm in an easy-to-read text that
incorporates phonics instruction and rebuses.
Includes bibliographical references (p. 16) and index.
  ISBN 0-7565-0516-X (hardcover : alk. paper)
  1. Domestic animals—Juvenile literature. 2. Reading—Phonetic
method—Juvenile literature. [1. Domestic animals. 2. Rebuses. 3.
Reading—Phonetic method.] I. Title. II. Series.
  SF75.5.C53 2003
  636—dc21   2003006362

Table of Contents

Dear Parent or Caregiver,

Welcome to Compass Point Phonics Readers, books of information for young children. Each book concentrates on specific phonic sounds and words commonly found in beginning reading materials. Featuring eye-catching photographs, every book explores a single science or social studies concept that is sure to grab a child's interest.

So snuggle up with your child, and let's begin. Start by reading aloud the Mother Goose nursery rhyme on the next page. As you read, stress the words in dark type. These are the words that contain the phonic sounds featured in this book. After several readings, pause before the rhyming words, and let your child chime in.

Now let's read *On a Farm*. If your child is a beginning reader, have him or her first read it silently. Then ask your child to read it aloud. For children who are not yet reading, read the book aloud as you run your finger under the words. Ask your child to imitate, or "echo," what he or she has just heard.

Discussing the book's content with your child:
Explain to your child that farms are places where different kinds of animals live and work. Animals are an important part of life on a farm. For example, cats catch mice, cows and goats give milk, and chickens lay eggs.

At the back of the book is a fun Tic-Tac-Toe game. Your child will take pride in demonstrating his or her mastery of the phonic sounds and the high-frequency words.

Enjoy Compass Point Phonics Readers and watch your child read and learn!

Hush-A-Bye

Hush-a-bye baby,
On the tree **top!**
When the wind blows,
The cradle will **rock;**
When the bough breaks,
The cradle will fall;
Down will come baby,
Cradle and all.

I see a fat .
What has it got?

I see a tan  cat .
It naps a lot.

I see a  COW .
It has spots.

I see a rabbit.
Hop! Hop! Hop!

I see a ⬚ pink ⬚ hog.
The hog is fat.

I see a  frog hop.
Plop! Plop! Plop!

I see a lot on a farm!

Word List

Short o

got
hog
hop
lot
on
plop
spots

g

got
hog

l

lot

p

hop
plop

High-Frequency

see
the

Social Studies

farm

Tic-Tac-Toe

Word Tic-Tac-Toe

pop	log	on
hop	the	spot
got	top	see

How to Play

- **Word Tic-Tac-Toe** Players take turns reading aloud a word and then covering it with a game piece. The first player to cover 3 words in a row down, across, or on the diagonal wins.
- **Letter Tic-Tac-Toe** Players take turns naming a letter, saying a word that begins with that letter (such as *d, dog*), and covering the letter. The first player to cover 3 letters in a row down, across, or on the diagonal wins.

Letter Tic-Tac-Toe

h	g	s
t	p	m
l	n	f

Read More

Longnecker, Theresa. *Who Grows Up on the Farm?: A Book About Farm Animals and Their Offspring.* Minneapolis, Minn.: Picture Window Books, 2003.

Roop, Peter, and Connie Roop. *A Farming Town.* Walk Around Series. Des Plaines, Ill.: Heinemann Library, 1999.

Schuh, Mari C. *Cats on the Farm.* Mankato, Minn.: Pebble Books, 2003.

Scott, Janine. *Farm Friends.* Minneapolis, Minn.: Compass Point Books, 2002.

Index